Construction Trucks
Activity Book

Victoria Allenby
Art by Peggy Collins

Printed in China by Qualibre Inc. / Print Plus

469 Richmond St. E, Toronto, ON M5A 1R1

Distributed in Canada by UTP Distribution
5201 Dufferin Street Toronto, Ontario Canada, M3H 5T8

Distributed in the U.S. by Ingram Publisher Services
1 Ingram Blvd. La Vergne, TN 37086, USA

Let's play SHAPES!

What can you draw using these shapes?

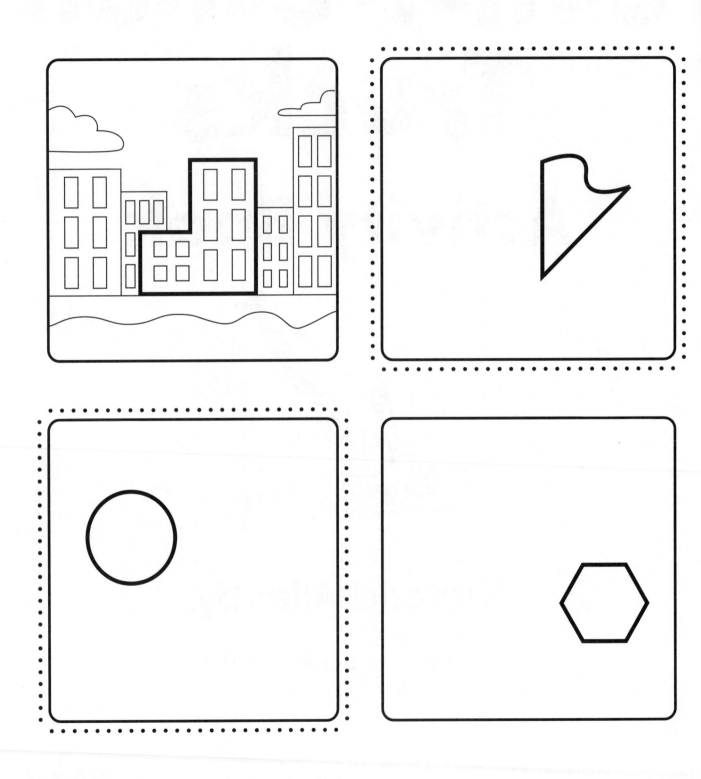

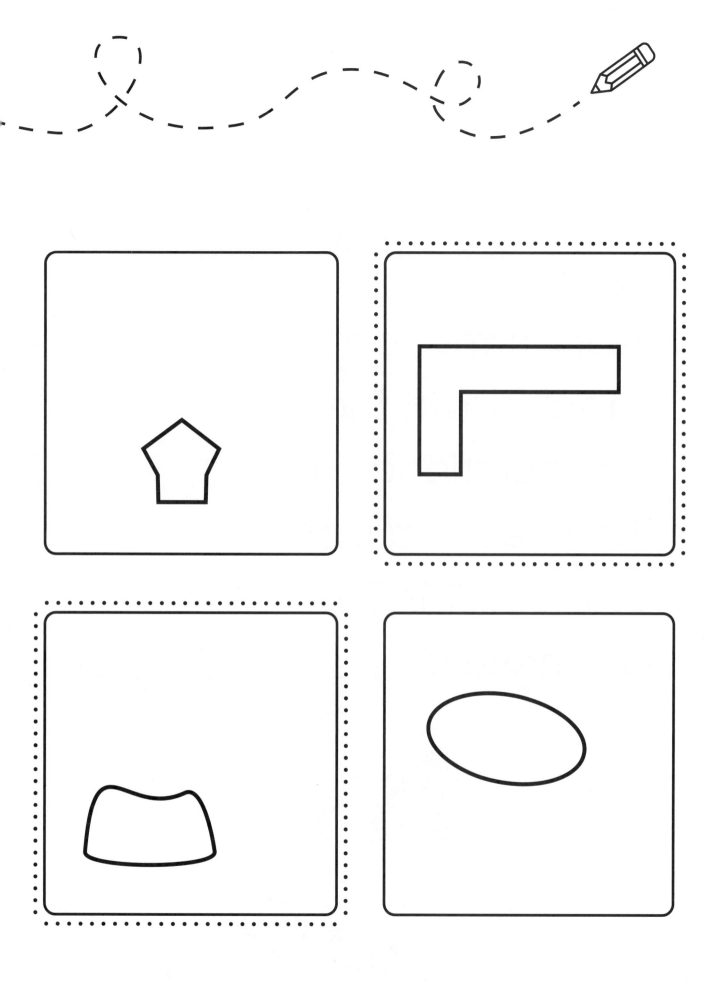

Complete the poem

Choose the rhyming word to complete the poem.

FLY   JUMP   FALL

Tear off the roof!

Knock down the wall!

Call our friend

The wrecking ball.

One big SMASH

Will make it _____!

Meet the Construction Engineer

The construction engineer manages whole building projects. They inspect designs, make sure the right materials are being used, and keep projects moving on time.

word search

BUILD   CITY   CRANE
LIFT   SKYSCRAPER

F S E J Q C
P H K G L I O
G N Y V I K K
E D S O F C D
B U C I T Y B
U H R Y M A N
I T A S R L X
L L P I J M F
D C E A W E P
B C R A N E Z Q

Let's solve the puzzle! 💡

Help the **forklift** deliver its box.

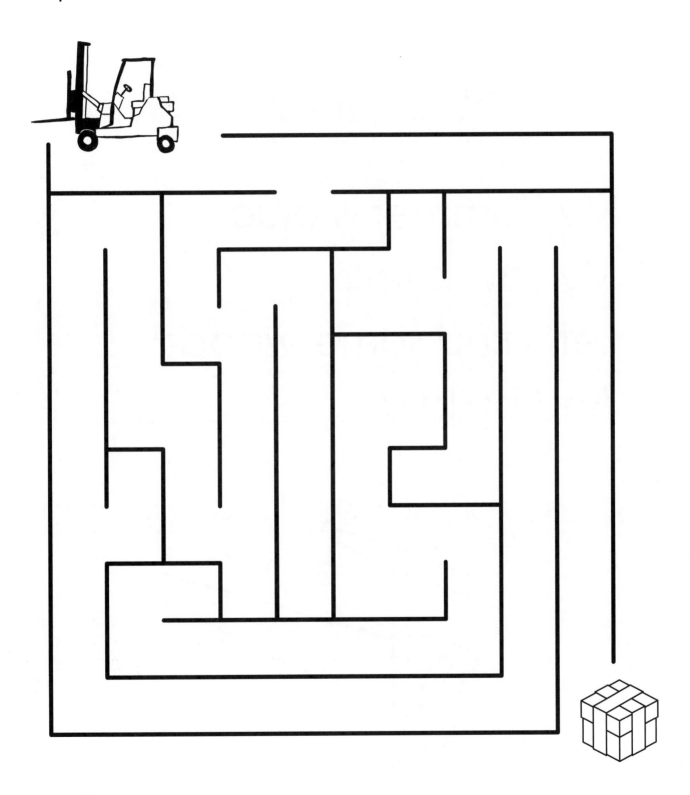

Complete the poem

Choose the rhyming word to complete the poem.

HOUSE   SHED   DESK

My hammer is blue.

My saw is red.

Let's find some wood

And build a _____!

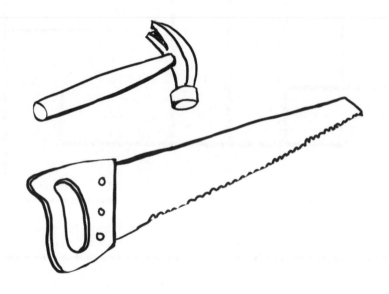

Meet the Construction Workers

Construction workers do many jobs. They use tools, direct traffic, spread concrete, take care of equipment, and much, much more!

Let's solve the puzzle! 💡

Solve the secret code.

⬭ = **A**	▢ = **R**	○ = **U**
▭ = **T**	☆ = **S**	◁ = **E**

W◁⬭R YO○R

☆⬭○F◁▭Y V◁☆▭!

Let's color!

Color the **front loader** and practice writing its name.

F R O N T   L O A D E R

Complete the silly story!

Choose each word from the box that matches the line.

Once there was a _____ dump truck

named _____ Joe. Joe was excited

to carry a lod of .... all the way

to _ _ _ _ _ _ _ _ _ _ _ _ _ _ _ _ _. On the way, Joe took

a wrong turn at ....Even worse, it

started to rain cats and ....! It was

～～～～～～～～～～～～～～～～ when Joe finally delivered his

load. He was ready for a _____ rest.

ADJECTIVES

- silly
- useful
- happy
- proud
- goofy
- foolish
- young
- long
- good

NOUNS

- worms
- jelly
- beans
- pigs
- bricks
- blankets
- chips
- dogs
- sand

PLACES

- the mayor's house
- the North Pole
- New York City
- Toronto
- Australia
- the railway station

TIMES

- 3 o'clock
- noon
- midnight
- 11 o'clock
- the next day

Let's play SHAPES!

What can you draw using these shapes?

Let's solve the puzzle!

Can you draw **one line** to turn this rectangle into **two triangles?**

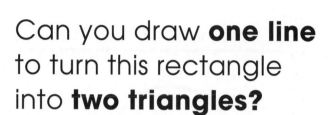

Can you draw **two lines** to turn this big square into **four small squares?**

Can you draw **two lines** to turn this trapezoid into **three triangles?**

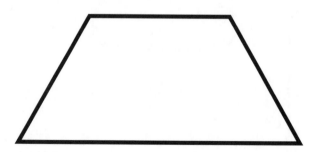

Meet the Foreman

The foreman is in charge of making sure everyone at a construction site knows what to do. The foreman can be any gender.

Scavenger Hunt

Can you spot these things the next time you are riding through town?

☐ A stop sign

☐ A yield sign

☐ A maintenance hole cover

☐ A vehicle with more than four wheels

☐ A vehicle with fewer than four wheels

☐ Someone wearing safety gear

Let's color!

Color the **excavator** and practice writing its name.

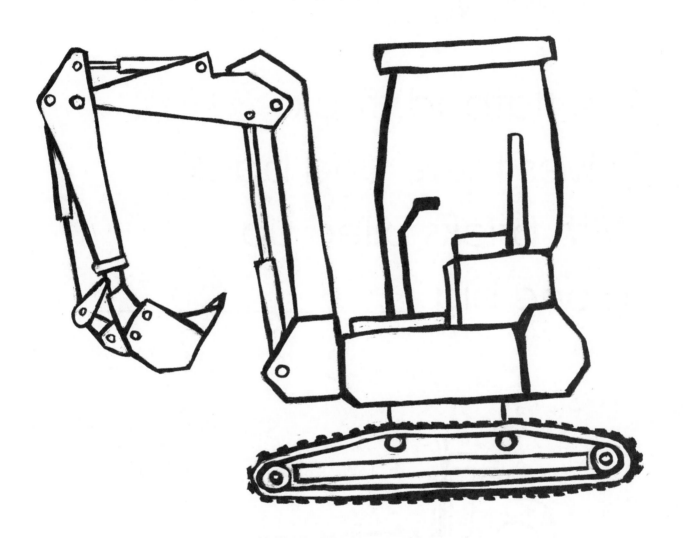

EXCAVATOR

Complete the poem

Choose the rhyming word to complete the poem.

STACK HILL TOWER

The flatbed truck

Drives there and back

With bricks piled up

In one big _____ .

Meet the Construction Inspector

The construction inspector makes sure that all safety rules are followed on a construction site.

Let's draw!

Draw the other half of the bulldozer.

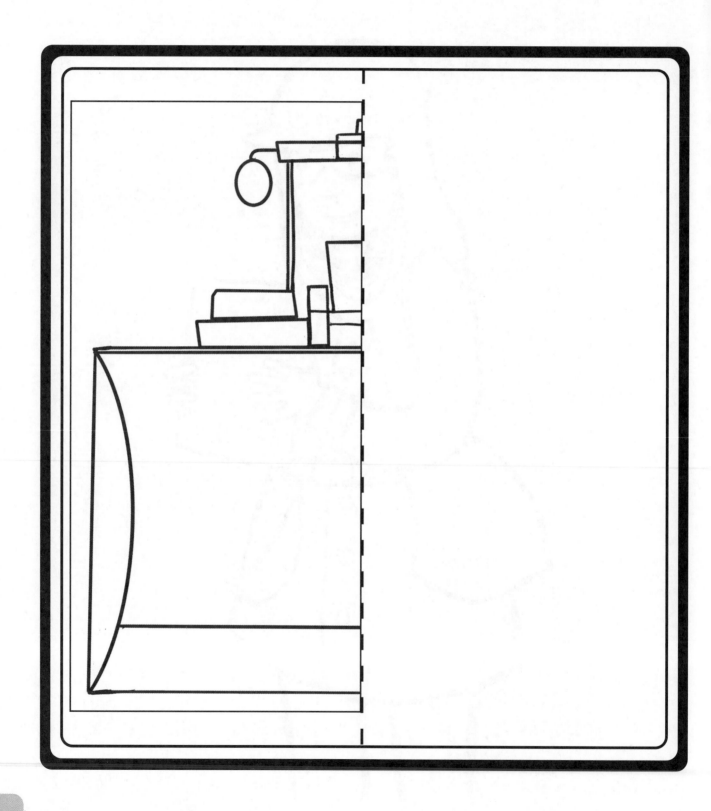

Let's match

Match the truck to its name.

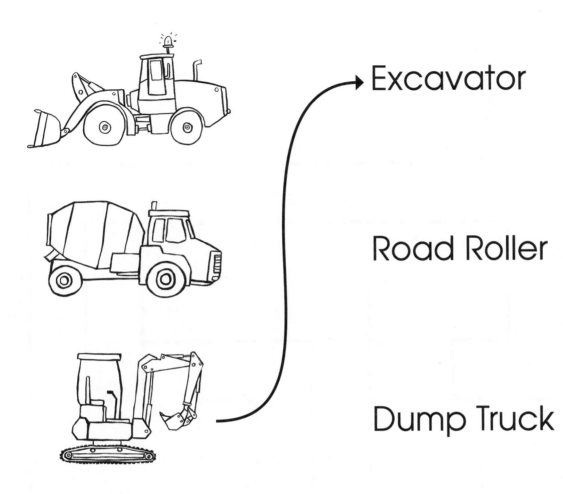

Excavator

Road Roller

Dump Truck

Front Loader

Concrete Mixer

Let's solve the puzzle!

Help the **dump truck** get through the town.

Construction Trucks

Heavy Lifting

A **mobile crane** can build...

...a **tower crane** in just one day.

Working Together

Can you spot
these shapes
in the picture?

Rectangle

Circle

The **excavator** digs up the earth.

The **dump truck** carries it away.

Trapezoid

Triangle

Construction Truck Travel

Caterpillar tracks help trucks move on loose surfaces like sand and gravel.

Wheels are good for packed-down surfaces.

When construction trucks have to travel on the highway, they catch a ride on a trailer.

HOW ARE Skyscrapers BUILT?

A **concrete mixer** fills a bucket with concrete...

...then a crane lifts the bucket to the top of the skyscraper.

Making

1. The **dump truck** pours asphalt

3. The **road roller** presses it down

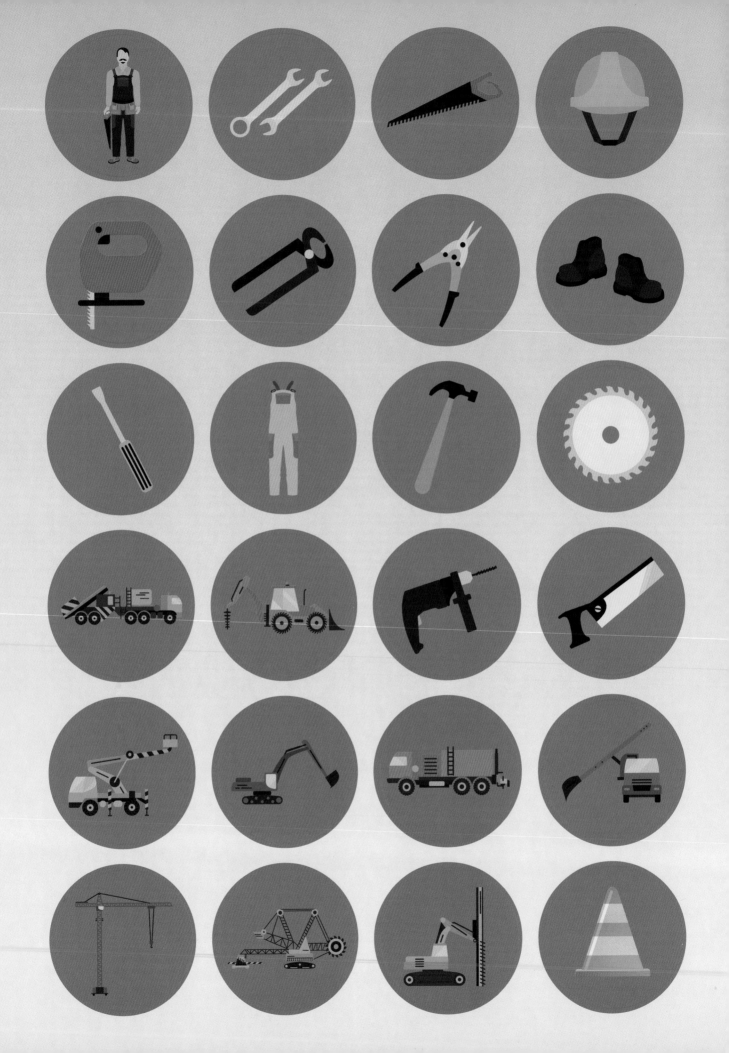

Roads

2.

The **asphalt paver** spreads it out

The **scribing machine** paints the lines

4.

Staying Safe

Safety gear must be worn by everyone at a construction site.

Workboots protect the feet from falling objects

Hard hats protect the head from falling objects

Headphones protect the ears from loud noises

Gloves keep the hands from being cut or scraped

Sturdy clothing is difficult to cut through by mistake

Harnesses are worn by anyone working up high

WHAT'S THE
Difference?

A bulldozer has a blade
at the front for pushing and digging

A front loader has a scoop
at the front for carrying dirt

HOW DO CONSTRUCTION TRUCKS HELP TEAR DOWN A BUILDING?

Wrecking balls
SMASH

Crushers
PULL

EXCAVATORS

KNOCK DOWN
& SCOOP UP

Dump trucks
CARRY AWAY

Big, Little Concept Books

PARENTAL GUIDE

Learning Shapes
A foundation for later math concepts

Rhyme & Rhythm
Encourage recitation, a first step to reading

Motor Skills
Practice tracing shapes with a finger

Family Reading, Ages 2–5
Read together to foster learning & development

Our sturdy formats include a parental guide highlighting the foundational learning skills they support

ISBN 978-1-77278-134-2
Hardcover
ISBN 978-1-77278-215-8
Board Book

NEW!

Victoria Allenby

ISBN 978-1-77278-213-4
Hardcover

NEW!
FOR 2022

Jane Whittingham

ISBN 978-1-177278-238-7
Hardcover

Coming in 2022

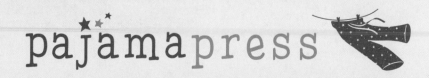

pajamapress

Let's solve the puzzle!

Find these shapes in the picture.

Let's solve the puzzle!

How many more hard hats are there than hammers?
Color the correct number.

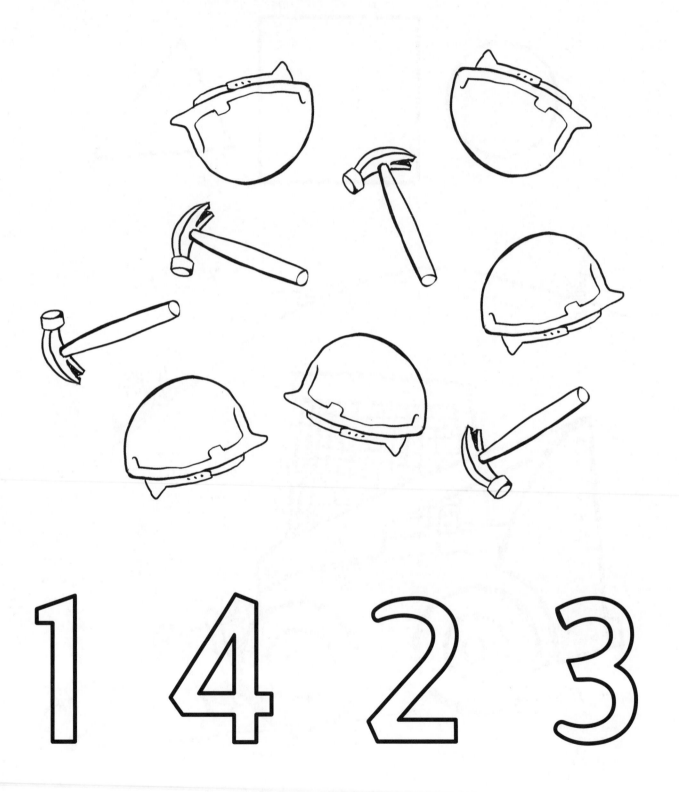

1 4 2 3

Let's draw!

Draw yourself driving the **road roller.**

Let's color!

Color the **dump truck** and practice writing its name.

DUMP TRUCK

Let's solve the puzzle!

Which crane is lifting the cupcakes?

Let's solve the puzzle!

Circle 5 differences in the pictures.

1 2 3 4 5

1 2 3 4 5

Let's solve the puzzle! 💡

Join the dots.

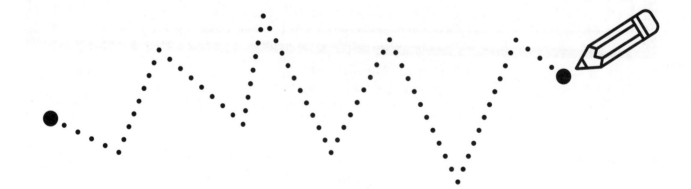

Let's color!

Color the **bucket truck** and practice writing its name.

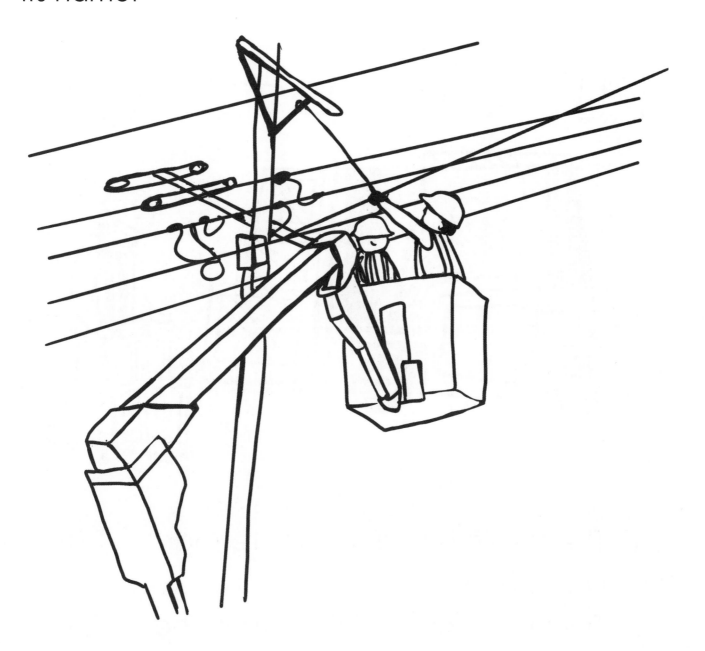

BUCKET TRUCK

True or False

Are these statements true or false?

1. The forklift is carrying more than two crates.   T / F

2. There are fewer hard hats in the picture than boots.   T / F

3. The number of crates is greater than the number of triangles.   T / F

Let's draw!

Learn to draw a **dump truck**.

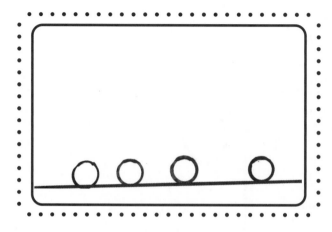

You draw!

word search

LOADER   WHEEL   DRIVE
CARRY   TRUCK

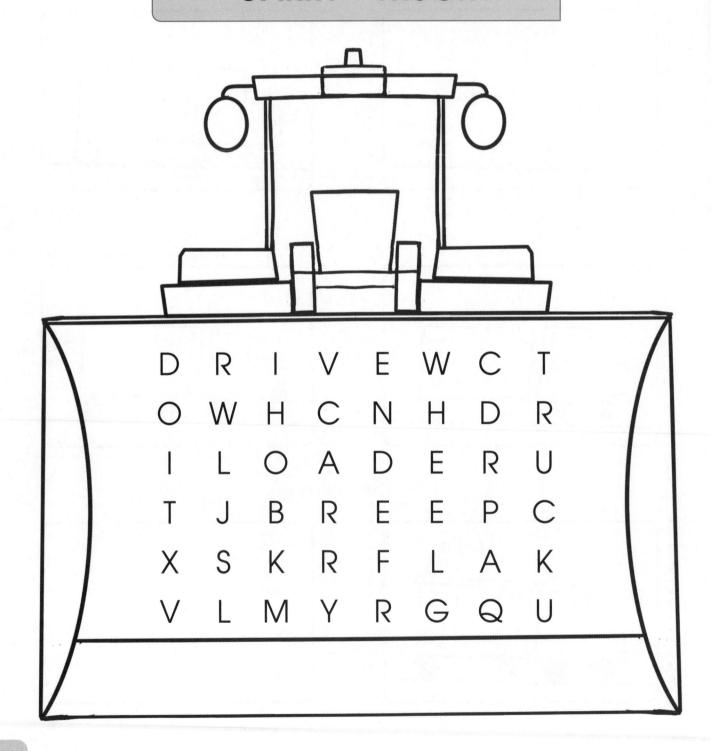

D R I V E W C T
O W H C N H D R
I L O A D E R U
T J B R E E P C
X S K R F L A K
V L M Y R G Q U

Let's draw!

Can you make a construction truck using 3 circles, a rectangle, and a square?

Let's solve the puzzle!

Use the code to color each section.
A secret picture will be revealed!

* = **RED**   — = **GREEN**

•• = **GREY**   ◁ = **BLACK**

Let's match

Match the truck to its shadow.

Let's solve the puzzle!

Find these shapes in the picture.

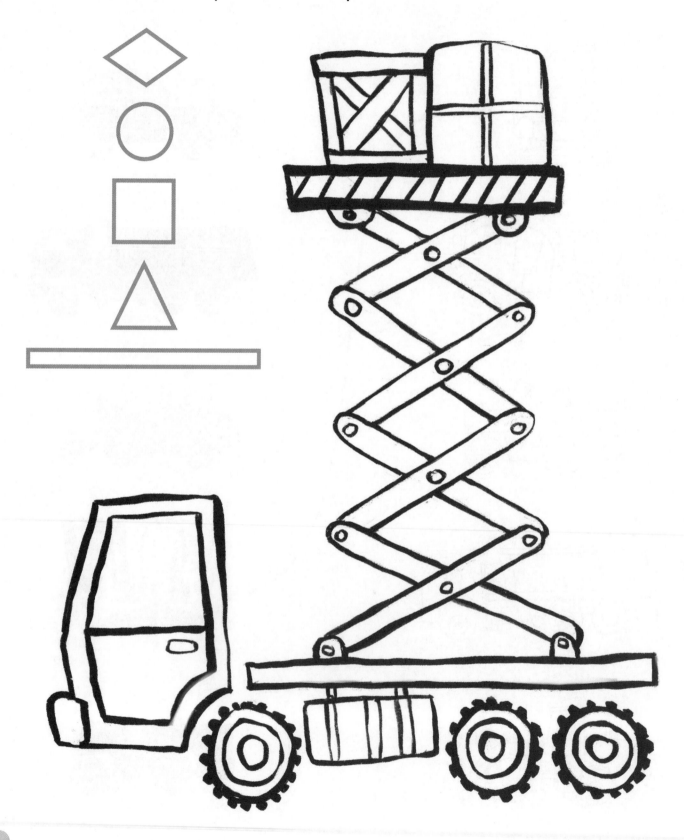

Let's color!

Color the **concrete mixer** and practice writing its name.

CONCRETE MIXER

Safety Gear

Construction workers wear special safety gear to protect themselves.

Gloves

Vest

Hard hat

Harness

Goggles

Work boots

Let's draw!

Draw safety gear onto the construction worker.

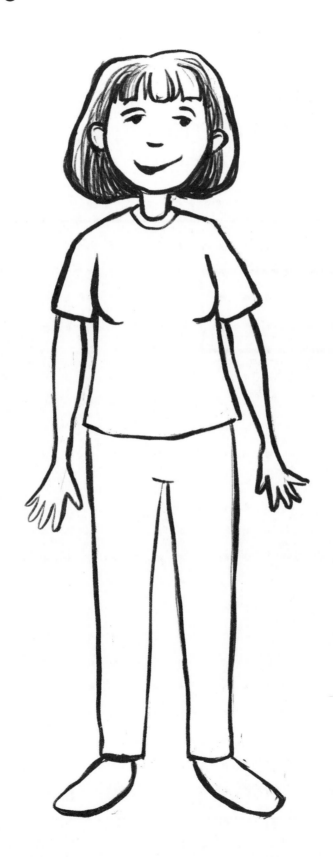

Let's solve the puzzle! 💡

Connect some dots to make these shapes:

- A triangle
- A rectangle
- A parallelogram
- A shape with 3 corners
- A shape with 5 corners

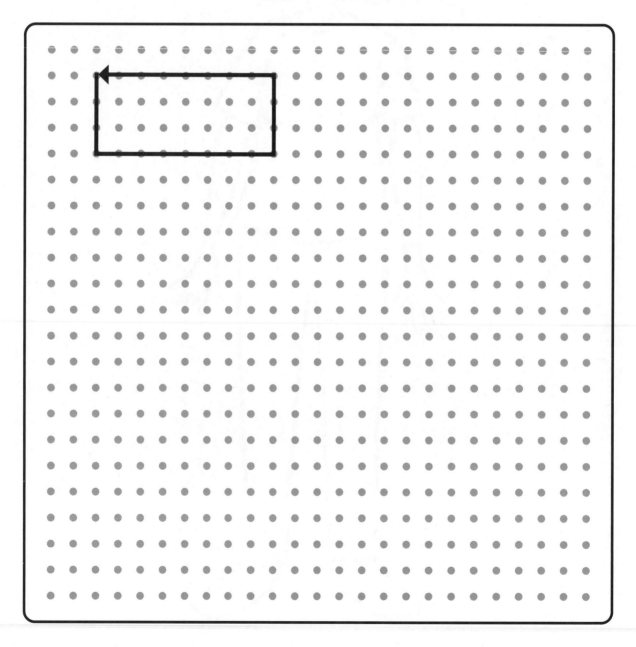

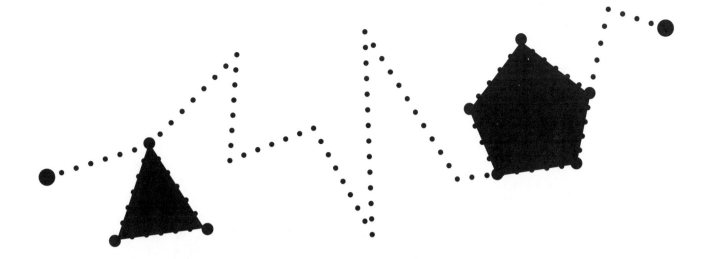

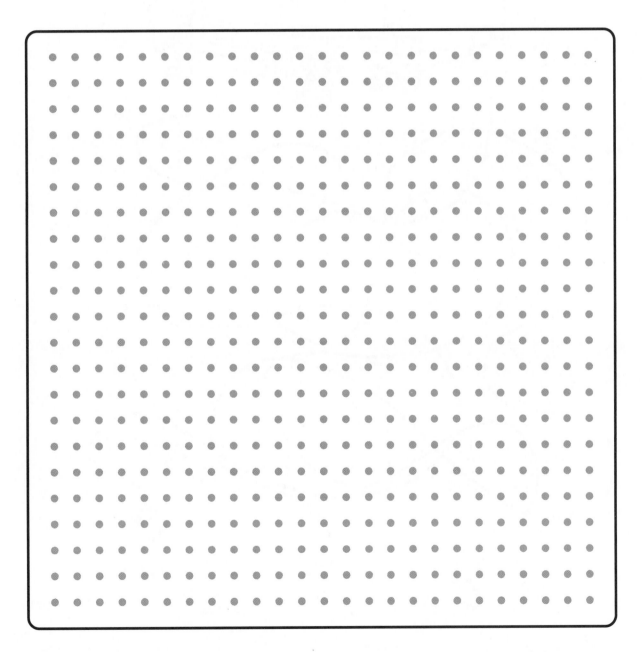

Let's solve the puzzle!

Which hook is attached to the winch?

Let's solve the puzzle!

Use the code to color each section.
A secret picture will be revealed!

1 = BROWN **2 = GREY** **3 = RED**

4 = GREEN **5 = BLACK** **6 = BLUE**

Let's solve the puzzle!

Join the dots.

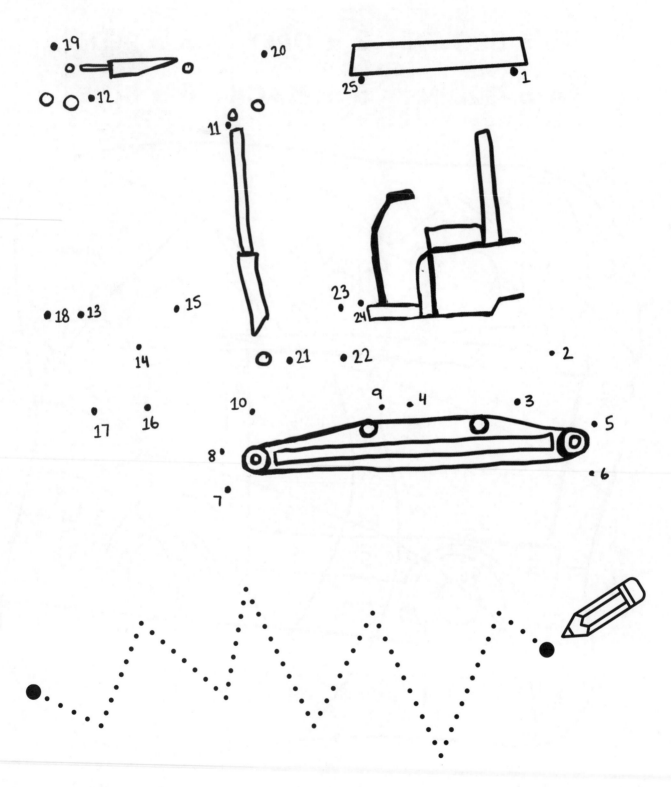